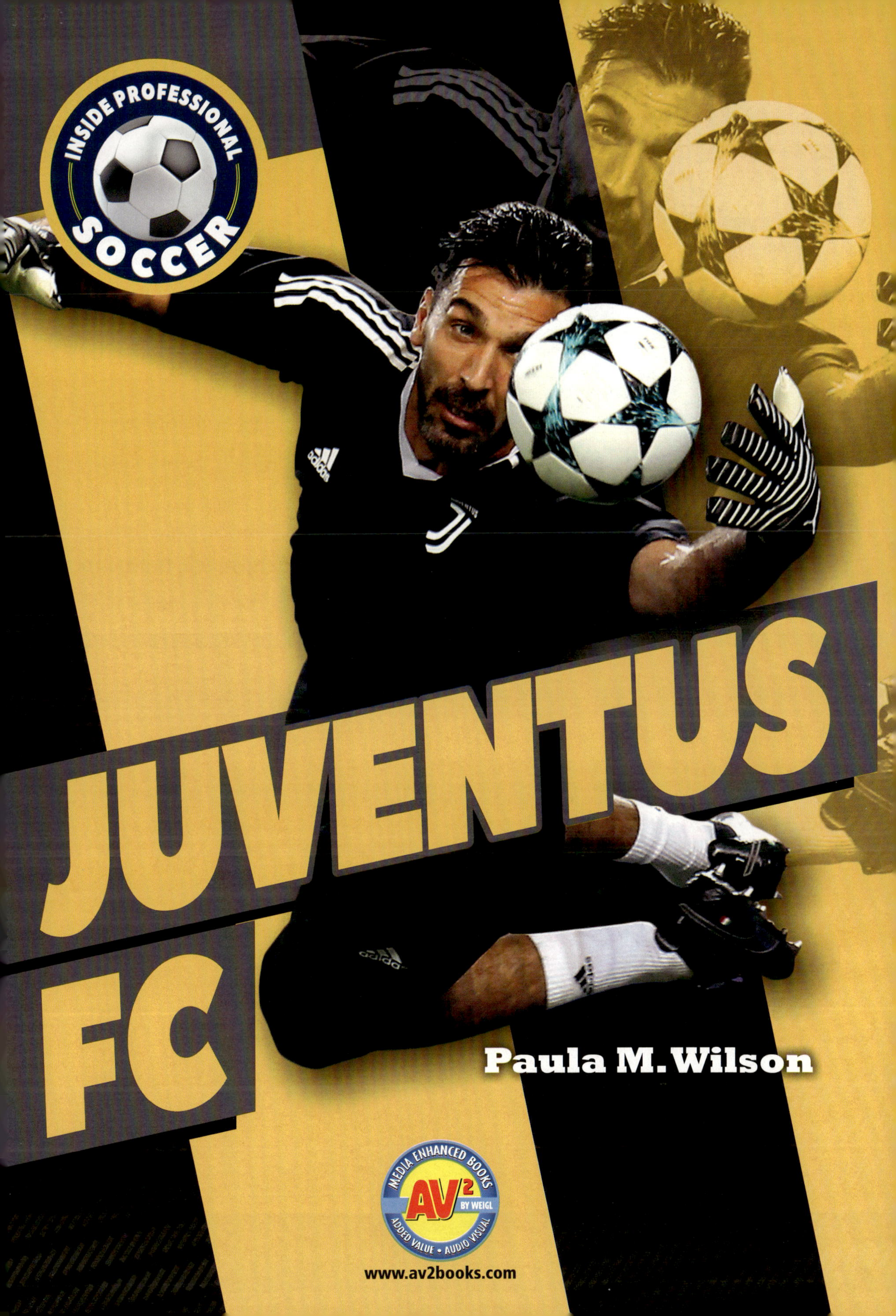

INSIDE PROFESSIONAL SOCCER

JUVENTUS FC

Paula M. Wilson

MEDIA ENHANCED BOOKS
AV2 BY WEIGL
ADDED VALUE • AUDIO VISUAL
www.av2books.com

Go to www.av2books.com, and enter this book's unique code.

BOOK CODE

AVW33648

AV² by Weigl brings you media enhanced books that support active learning.

AV² provides enriched content that supplements and complements this book. Weigl's AV² books strive to create inspired learning and engage young minds in a total learning experience.

Your AV² Media Enhanced books come alive with...

Audio
Listen to sections of the book read aloud.

Key Words
Study vocabulary, and complete a matching word activity.

Video
Watch informative video clips.

Quizzes
Test your knowledge.

Embedded Weblinks
Gain additional information for research.

Slide Show
View images and captions, and prepare a presentation.

Try This!
Complete activities and hands-on experiments.

... and much, much more!

Published by AV² by Weigl
350 5th Avenue, 59th Floor
New York, NY 10118
Website: www.av2books.com

Library of Congress Control Number: 2018930411

ISBN 978-1-4896-7793-8 (hardcover)
ISBN 978-1-4896-7794-5 (softcover)
ISBN 978-1-4896-7795-2 (multi-user eBook)

Printed in the United States of America in Brainerd, Minnesota
1 2 3 4 5 6 7 8 9 0 22 21 20 19 18

022018
120817

Project Coordinator: John Willis   Designer: Terry Paulhus

The publisher acknowledges Getty Images, Alamy, Shutterstock, and Wikimedia as its primary image suppliers for this title.

INSIDE PROFESSIONAL SOCCER

CONTENTS

Introduction

A group of kids in Turin, Italy, started the Juventus Football Club. They would be thrilled to see how the team has developed into a world-class soccer **powerhouse.** Turin is a city in northern Italy, very close to the borders of France and Switzerland. The city is in the shadow of the mountain range called the **Alps**.

Soccer is also known as football in many countries. In Italy, competition is fierce among the dozens of professional soccer teams. However, Juventus continues to finish at the top of the division season after season. They have won the **Scudetto** and the **Coppa Italia** more than any other team in Italian soccer history.

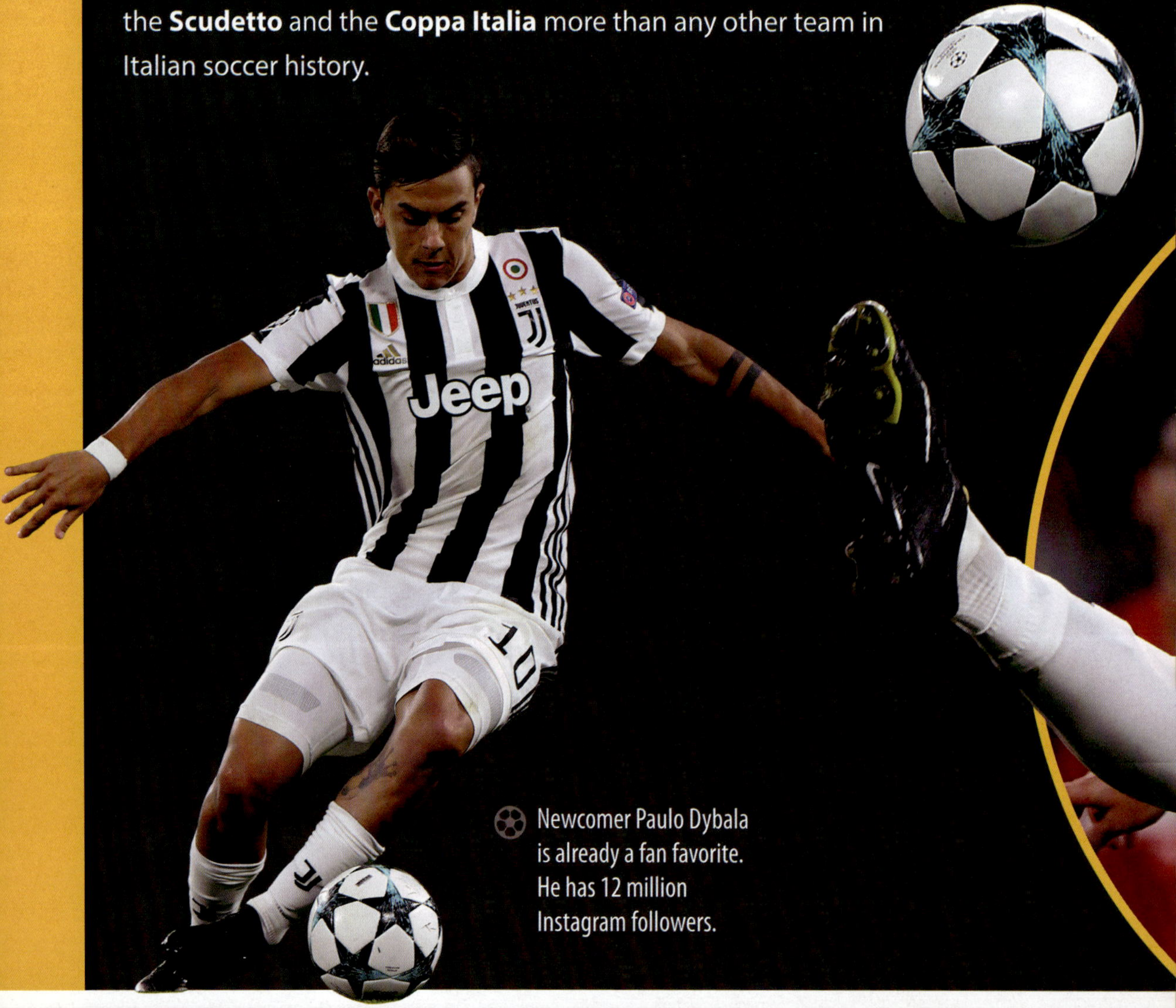

Newcomer Paulo Dybala is already a fan favorite. He has 12 million Instagram followers.

Some consider Juventus to be the best **Serie A** soccer team of all time. The team invests millions of dollars to attract the world's best players to Turin. Juve's **roster** is full of these powerful and talented players. They hope to continue to be leaders in the world of soccer.

With 38 goals in the 2016-17 season, Gonzalo Higuaín is doing his part to keep Juventus at the top of the league.

JUVENTUS FC

Arena Allianz Stadium

Division Serie A Division

Head Coach Massimiliano Allegri

Location Turin, Italy

FIFA Club World Cups 0

Nicknames Juve, *la Vecchia Signora* ("the Old Lady"), *Bianconeri* ("White and Black")

65 Trophies and cups

2 UEFA Super Cups

8 million Instagram followers

165,000 Juventus Museum visitors per year

130,000 Record single-game attendance

History

Juventus is one of the oldest soccer clubs in Italy.

In 1897, a group of students decided to start a soccer club. They were from the Massimo D'Azeglio school in Turin, Italy. The oldest boy was only 17 years old, so they called themselves *Juventus*, which means "youth" in Latin. A few years later, they played in their first national championship. Then, in 1905, just eight years after the boys started Juventus, they won their first Scudetto.

By 1923, the team had made a name for itself among local fans in Turin. They were bought by the Agnelli family, who owned the nearby FIAT car company. With financial support from their new owners, the team was able to sign star players to their roster. This paved the way for future success.

Year after year, Juve succeeded in bringing home league championships. Today, they have a total of 33. Several outstanding players and coaches led the team to success over the last 120 years. Players such as Roberto Baggio, Giampiero Boniperti, and Alessandro Del Piero have a special place in Juventus history. Their skill on the **pitch** gave them the ability to win important games.

Nine players from Juventus were on the Italian national soccer team that won the 1934 World Cup. It was the first World Cup win by Italy.

The Arena

Well-known **Juve players' names** are engraved into cement **stars** around the stadium.

Allianz Stadium is the sixth largest stadium in Italy.

Juventus has called Turin, Italy, its home since its first day in 1897. The field where the original squad started was called *Piazza d'Armi*, or "Parade Ground." From there, the team played in other Turin stadiums including the *Stadio Comunale*, the "Municipal Stadium," and the *Stadio delle Alpi*, the "Stadium of the Alps." Juve called Stadio Comunale home for 57 years, longer than any other stadium. The team won 17 Scudetto titles there.

On September 8, 2011, Juventus opened a brand-new home, now called the Allianz Stadium. It was built on the grounds of the old Stadio delle Alpi. In the new arena, every seat has a clear view of the pitch. The first row of seats is only 24 feet (7.5 meters) from the playing field.

The stadium was built in an eco-friendly way. Solar energy is used to heat the stadium. There is also a system to catch rainwater for reuse. The builders recycled the concrete from the old stadium to build the new structure.

The Juventus Museum has a trophy room filled with the team's cups and trophies for fans to see.

Where They Play

Arena
Allianz Stadium

Location
Corso Gaetano Scirea, 50,
10151 Turin, Italy

Broke Ground
2009

Completed
September 8, 2011

Field Design
Two soaring arches anchor each end of the stadium. The arches, colored red, green, and white for the Italian flag, can be seen for miles across the Turin skyline.

Features
- 41,500 seats
- 16 suspended walkways into the stadium
- Juventus Museum and stadium tours

SERIE A DIVISION TEAMS

1	Atalanta *(Bergamo, Italy)*	★ 11	Juventus *(Turin, Italy)*
2	Benevento *(Benevento, Italy)*	12	Lazio *(Rome, Italy)*
3	Bologna *(Bologna, Italy)*	13	Milan *(Milan, Italy)*
4	Cagliari *(Cagliari, Italy)*	14	Napoli *(Naples, Italy)*
5	Chievo *(Verona, Italy)*	15	Roma *(Rome, Italy)*
6	Crotone *(Crotone, Italy)*	16	Sampdoria *(Genoa, Italy)*
7	Fiorentina *(Florence, Italy)*	17	Sassuolo *(Sassuolo, Italy)*
8	Genoa *(Genoa, Italy)*	18	SPAL *(Ferrara, Italy)*
9	Hellas Verona *(Verona, Italy)*	19	Torino *(Turin, Italy)*
10	Inter Milan *(Milan, Italy)*	20	Udinese *(Udine, Italy)*

The Uniforms

In 2016, Juventus fans bought about 850,000 uniforms to support their favorite team and players.

The players who started Juventus in 1897 wore short-sleeved pink shirts. Six years later, the team needed new shirts. One of the players arranged to have jerseys sent to Italy from the Notts County soccer team in Great Britain. Notts County sent a set of jerseys with black-and-white stripes. Today, the Juventus and Notts County soccer clubs both wear black and white. When Juventus players are away from their home stadium, they wear yellow **kits**.

The Juventus team kits have three gold stars above the team logo. Each star represents 10 national titles won by the team. In 2017, the team updated their logo. Instead of using a crest shape, the team now uses a stylized "J." The new, simple logo design is more modern-looking than the team's traditional crest.

In 2017, to celebrate their 120th anniversary, Juventus designed a limited-edition jersey. It is similar to jerseys of the past.

Goalie Gear

Goalie gloves have gotten larger over the years, with more padding to protect goalkeepers' hands.

It is easy to pick out the **goalkeepers** in soccer. They wear a different-colored jersey from their teammates. Juventus goalkeepers do not wear black-and-white striped shirts. Instead, they wear a solid color. This color has changed over the years. Recently, bright orange, green, or blue are the colors of choice for Juventus keepers.

Unlike other professional sports goalies, soccer keepers do not usually wear any special body padding or helmets. They are allowed to wear gloves to protect their hands. The gloves also give them additional grip when handling the ball.

Juventus fans celebrate their beloved goalie, Gianluigi Buffon, by calling him "Superman," and for good reason. For 16 years, he has been a fixture in the Juve goal, helping the team rack up win after win. Thanks to his unmatched talent, he was awarded best goalkeeper of the year by the Fédération Internationale de Football Association (FIFA) in 2017.

Gianluigi Buffon played his 1,000th professional game during the 2016–2017 season.

The Coaches

Massimiliano Allegri spent his playing career in Italy as a midfielder. He retired in 2003 and began his coaching career with Aglianese the following season.

Giovanni Trapattoni is the first coach in European soccer to win all three European championships with one team. He guided Juve to the European Cup, UEFA Cup, and the UEFA Cup Winner's Cup.

The job of guiding a team on the field is no easy task. However, some Juventus coaches have had exactly what it takes to get their players to deliver wins. Most of Juve's coaches stayed for just a year or two. The coaches who stayed longer are a big part of why the team has been able to stay at the top of the league.

GIOVANNI TRAPATTONI Giovanni Trapattoni, or "Trap" for short, began his soccer career on the field. He was a successful player before moving on to coaching. As a coach, Trapattoni made a name for himself as a skilled and effective leader. In his more than 10 years at the helm, he guided Juventus to six league championships.

MASSIMILIANO ALLEGRI Massimiliano Allegri has been the coach of Juve since 2014. Through his leadership, he has positioned the team for continued success. Under his guidance, Juve has won three **consecutive** "doubles." This means they won the Serie A league and the Coppa Italia in the same year. Fans are hoping he can extend the winning streak in years to come.

ANTONIO CONTE Antonio Conte played midfield with Juventus for 13 years before becoming their coach in 2011. His leadership earned him the Golden Bench award three years in a row. The award honors the best coach in the Serie A league. Conte led the team to three Serie A cups in a row and two back-to-back Coppa Italia wins.

Fans Around the World

The mascot for Juventus is a Zebra named Jay. His stripes match the Juventus jerseys.

Juventus enjoys the support of its fiercely loyal fans. Soccer is part of Italian culture. Team loyalties go back for generations. Juventus fans love their *Bianconeri*, an affectionate name for Juventus that means "black and white." The striped jerseys are a symbol of pride among fans. On game day, the stands are full of people wearing the team's colors.

Juventus is the pride of Turin, Italy. However, the team has an enormous following around the globe as well. There are official fan clubs on six of the seven continents, including clubs in countries as far away as Japan, Indonesia, and Australia. These worldwide fans connect with each other through the official Juve app and on social media platforms such as Facebook, where the team has 30 million followers.

Fan Traditions

#1 Whether in the stands at Allianz Stadium or cheering from home, fans wave black-and-white striped scarves to show their support for Juve.

#2 Before each home match, fans proclaim their support for Juve with the team's theme song, "Tale of Great Love."

Legends of the Past

Many great players have suited up for Juventus FC. A few of them have become icons of the team and the city it represents.

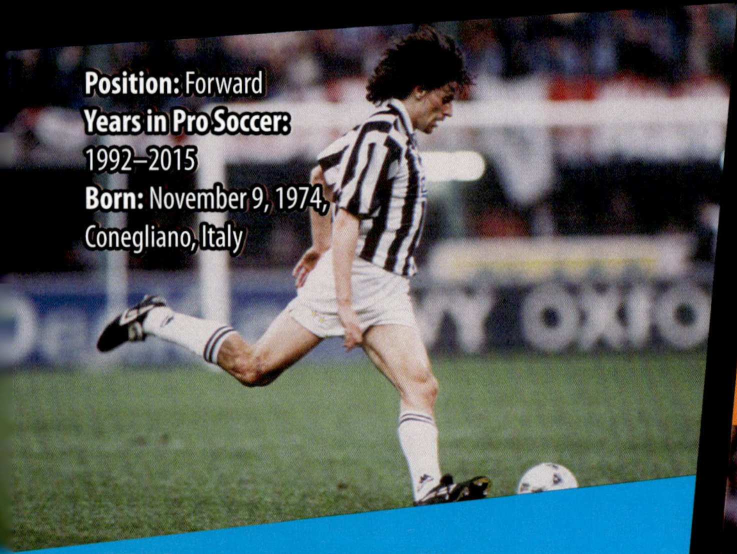

Position: Forward
Years in Pro Soccer: 1992–2015
Born: November 9, 1974, Conegliano, Italy

Alessandro Del Piero

Forward Alessandro Del Piero signed with Juventus on June 28, 1993. It was not long before his style and technical skill on the pitch set him apart as one of the best players the team ever had. Del Piero made his number 10 jersey very well known. He is considered a hero among Juventus fans because of his athleticism and his ability to make critical, game-winning plays. In 2006, Del Piero broke a 40-year record to become the all-time highest scorer for Juventus. This record still stands today. His career with Juventus spanned an incredible 19 years and 705 games.

Pavel Nedvěd

A fan favorite, Pavel Nedvěd played for Juve from 2001 to 2009. In that time, the midfielder played 214 Serie A games and scored 40 goals. He was known for his powerful shots, speed, and stamina. In 2003, Nedvěd was awarded the Golden Ball for being the best player of the year. His performance in the midfield helped Juve bring home the Scudetto four times. Nedvěd contributed his soccer skills to the Czech national team for much of his career. He retired from Juventus in 2009 but returned in 2015 to become vice president of the team.

Position: Midfield
Years in Pro Soccer: 1991–2009
Born: August 30, 1972, Cheb, Czechoslovakia

Roberto Baggio

Roberto Baggio is known as the "Divine Ponytail" because of his hairstyle. He started his career in Serie A with the Italian team Fiorentina. Baggio moved to Juventus in 1990 and quickly became known as one of the best forwards in the game. He is credited with many game-changing goals. His speed, ball-handling skills, and goal-scoring ability helped Juve win the Scudetto in 1995 and the UEFA Cup in 1993. In Baggio's five seasons with Juventus, he played in a total of 141 games and scored 78 goals. Baggio left Juventus in 1995, moving on to play for AC Milan.

Position: Forward
Years in Pro Soccer: 1982–2004
Born: February 18, 1967, Caldogno, Italy

Giampiero Boniperti

Giampiero Boniperti is a Juventus goal-scoring legend. He played on the black-and-white squad for his entire career. Boniperti is considered one of the most valuable players in Juve history. He racked up a record-setting 179 goals in his 459 appearances. His record held up for 40 years. Boniperti's power and technical skills helped Juventus bring home five Scudetto wins and two Coppa Italia championships during his 15 years with the team.

Position: Forward
Years in Pro Soccer: 1946–1961
Born: July 4, 1928, Barengo, Italy

Stars of Today

Today's Juventus FC team is made up of many young, talented players who have proven that they are among the best in the league.

Gianluigi Buffon

Gianluigi Buffon has played for Juventus since 2001. The only other team he has played for during his long career is Parma. He is considered one of the best goalkeepers of all time. The 6 foot 3 inches (175 centimeters) goalkeeper and team captain is legendary for his consistent agility and command of the goal area. In the 2015–16 season, Buffon set the Italian soccer league record for going the longest without having a goal scored against him. He lasted 973 minutes. Buffon has eight Scudetto titles under his belt. That is more than any other Serie A goalkeeper.

Position: Goalkeeper
Years in Pro Soccer: 1995–present
Born: January 28, 1978, Carrara, Italy

Gonzalo Higuaín

Gonzalo Higuaín started his first season with Juve by helping the squad bring home the league championship. He scored 36 goals in that first season. This broke a record that had stood since 1950. Higuaín is best known for his goal-scoring ability and his ball-handling skills. He earned himself a spot on the Argentinian national team in 2010 and 2014. He has appeared in 33 World Cup matches, scoring 16 goals. Before joining Juventus, Higuaín played for the team's rival, Napoli.

Position: Forward
Years in Pro Soccer: 2004–present
Born: December 10, 1987, Brest, France

Paulo Dybala

Paulo Dybala played his first season with Juventus in 2015. That season, he scored 23 goals, making him the team's leading scorer for the season. This rising star did not slow down the following season. Instead, he helped Juve to yet another league championship. Dybala's speed, ball control, and goal-scoring accuracy are what set him apart from other players on the pitch. Before joining Juventus, Dybala played for three years on the Italian squad Palermo. He is also a member of Argentina's national soccer team. Dybala's nickname is *la Hoya*, meaning "the Jewel," because of his standout talent and value to the team.

Position: Forward
Years in Pro Soccer: 2011–present
Born: November 15, 1993, Laguna Larga, Argentina

Giorgio Chiellini

Giorgio Chiellini came to Juventus in 2005 from rival Italian club Fiorentina. His leadership and powerful defense of the Juve goal make Chiellini an asset to the team. The 6 foot 1 inch (185 cm) **defender** helped the team achieve success with a string of six Serie A league championships and three Coppa Italia wins. Chiellini was a member of the Italian national soccer team until 2017. He played in World Cup matches for more than 10 years.

Position: Defender
Years in Pro Soccer: 2000–present
Born: August 14, 1984, Pisa, Italy

All-Time Records

6
Most straight Scudetto wins
No other team has called the championship theirs for six consecutive years. Starting in 2012 and running through 2017, Juventus kept the championship in Turin.

22
Most shutouts in a season
Juventus's goalkeeping and defense shut down their opponents in 22 games in both the 2013–14 and 2015–16 seasons.

105
Most Shutouts
Not much gets by Gianluigi Buffon. In his 16 years and counting with Juventus, Buffon has kept the ball out of the net in 105 matches.

290

Most Goals Scored

Alessandro Del Piero's goal-scoring ability was unmatched, finding the net 290 times in his 19 years with Juve.

33

Total Scudetto wins

Juve sits on top of the league with the most championships in the history of the Serie A division.

Timeline

Throughout the team's history, Juventus FC has had many memorable events that have become defining moments for the team and its fans.

1897
Juventus Football Club is established in Turin, Italy, by a group of boys from the Massimo D'Azeglio school.

1938
Juventus wins their first Coppa Italia.

1890 1900 1910 1920 1930 1940 1950

1923
The Agnelli family, owners of the FIAT car company, takes ownership of Juventus.

1930–1935
Juventus wins the Scudetto five years in a row.

In 1901, the team makes its first appearance in a national championship game.

1958
Juventus wins their 10th Scudetto, which earns them the right to wear a gold star on their uniforms.

1982
The Scudetto title goes to Juventus for the 20th time. The team can now wear a second gold star on their jerseys.

2003
The team enters into an agreement with the city of Turin to build a new stadium on the site of the aging Stadio delle Alpi.

2006
Juventus is caught up in a match-fixing scandal. The team has to play in a lower league for the 2006-2007 season, and they are stripped of their 2005 and 2006 championship titles.

In 2015, Juventus wins their 10th Coppa Italia.

The Future
One of Italy's oldest and most successful soccer teams, Juventus does not disappoint its fans. Their skill and style of play is world class, and they do not seem to be slowing down. With six league championships in a row, an impressive roster, and a skilled coach, the future looks very exciting for Juventus.

1960 | 1970 | 1980 | 1990 | 2000 | 2010 | 2020

Write a Biography

Life Story

A person's life story can be the subject of a book. This kind of book is called a biography. Biographies often describe the lives of people who have achieved great success. These people may be alive today, or they may have lived many years ago. Reading a biography can help you learn more about a great person.

Get the Facts

Use this book, and research in the library and on the internet, to find out more about your favorite player. Learn as much about him as you can. What position does he play? What are his statistics in important categories? Has he set any records? Also, be sure to write down key events in the person's life. What was his childhood like? What has he accomplished off the field? Is there anything else that makes this person special or unusual?

Use the Concept Web

A concept web is a useful research tool. Read the questions in the concept web on the following page. Answer the questions in your notebook. Your answers will help you write a biography.

Concept Web

Write a Biography

Adulthood
- Where does this individual currently reside?
- Does he or she have a family?

Your Opinion
- What did you learn from the books you read in your research?
- Would you suggest these books to others?
- Was anything missing from these books?

Childhood
- Where and when was this person born?
- Describe his or her parents, siblings, and friends.
- Did this person grow up in unusual circumstances?

Accomplishments off the Field
- What is this person's life's work?
- Has he or she received awards or recognition for accomplishments?
- How have this person's accomplishments served others?

Help and Obstacles
- Did this individual have a positive attitude?
- Did he or she receive help from others?
- Did this person have a mentor?
- Did this person face any hardships?
- If so, how were the hardships overcome?

Accomplishments on the Field
- What records does this person hold?
- What key games and plays have defined his career?
- What are his stats in categories important to his position?

Work and Preparation
- What was this person's education?
- What was his or her work experience?
- How does this person work?
- What is the process he or she uses?

Trivia Time

Take this quiz to test your knowledge of Juventus FC. The answers are printed upside down under each question.

1 What year did the team's brand-new stadium open?

A. 2011

2 What color were the original shirts worn by Juventus?

A. Pink

3 How many Serie A Championships has the team won?

A. 33

4 The team is from what city?

A. Turin

5 Who scored the most goals in team history?

A. Alessandro Del Piero

6 How many national titles does a team need to win to wear a gold star on their jerseys?

A. 10

7 Which team nickname means "black and white"?

A. Bianconeri

8 What does the word *Juventus* mean?

A. "Youth"

9 How many gold stars do Juventus players wear on their jerseys?

A. Three

Key Words

Alps: a mountain range in Europe

consecutive: following one after another in a series

Coppa Italia: the Italian cup

defender: also called a back. A player who plays in front of the goal and stops the other team from scoring.

forward: a player on a soccer team who normally plays closest to the opponent's goal

goalkeepers: also called goalies. The players responsible for keeping the ball from going into the goal and the only players who are allowed to pick up the ball.

kits: standard attire and equipment worn by soccer players, including shirts, shorts, socks, and shin guards

pitch: an area that is used for playing sports

powerhouse: a person, group, or thing that has great energy or strength

roster: a list of players who belong to a particular team

Scudetto: the award given to the champions of Italy's top division of professional soccer

Serie A: the top professional soccer league in Italy

Index

Log on to www.av2books.com

AV² by Weigl brings you media enhanced books that support active learning. Go to www.av2books.com, and enter the special code found on page 2 of this book. You will gain access to enriched and enhanced content that supplements and complements this book. Content includes video, audio, weblinks, quizzes, a slide show, and activities.

AV² Online Navigation

Audio
Listen to sections of the book read aloud.

Book Pages
AV² pages directly correspond to pages in the book.

Video
Watch informative video clips.

Embedded Weblinks
Gain additional information for research.

Key Words
Study vocabulary, and complete a matching word activity.

Try This!
Complete activities and hands-on experiments.

Quizzes
Test your knowledge.

Slide Show
View images and captions, and prepare a presentation.

AV² was built to bridge the gap between print and digital. We encourage you to tell us what you like and what you want to see in the future.

Sign up to be an AV² Ambassador at www.av2books.com/ambassador.

Due to the dynamic nature of the Internet, some of the URLs and activities provided as part of AV² by Weigl may have changed or ceased to exist. AV² by Weigl accepts no responsibility for any such changes. All media enhanced books are regularly monitored to update addresses and sites in a timely manner. Contact AV² by Weigl at 1-866-649-3445 or av2books@weigl.com with any questions, comments, or feedback.